Vulnerable **AF**

Vulnerable **AF**

— poems —

TARRIONA "TANK" BALL

Andrews McMeel
PUBLISHING®

A collection of poems so that I can remember . . . and forget

Dedicated to the boy with the deepest mud puddles
I have ever stepped in

Tank's Story Time

"You Don't Know Shit About Shit, Maw"

I used to work at a nursing home. My job included sitting for
hours and answering the few calls they would get. With so much
time on my hands, I'd read the romance novels they kept at the
nursing home to keep wandering minds at bay and give hope
to the hopeless romantics. That was my favorite part of the job.
Reading. There were so many books, and I loved reimagining
those love stories over and over in my head. I wanted to be in
love. I fantasized and romanticized it more than I should have.
Infatuation ain't nothing nice for any girl of any age, especially
one in her early twenties with no experience to counter those
exaggerated feelings. My Infatuation led me to believe that I was
in actual love with someone I barely knew. The can't-eat-can't-
think-can't-sleep type of love. But I kept thinking, writing. I
wondered, I wandered, I hoped, I wanted, I lusted, and I thought I
knew. What I found was that you sometimes get exactly what you
are looking for, and sometimes that thing finds you.

Know

I once heard someone say if you read Tarriona's poetry
You will know that she has never been in love
I wonder if they listened closely
They would know . . .
That I wanted to be

Tank's Story Time

Playing Hard to Get

You ever been with someone who was super affectionate when
no one was around? What about somebody who never wanted to
hold your hand in public? Or only complimented you when no one
could hear? Yeah, that was him.

I'm pretty confident saying that I grew up with a lot of odds
against me. I was short, dark skinned, no hips, no big booty, fat
. . . But I still had people around me who made me feel beautiful.
Those particular people were my sisters. Not too many men,
though. I had the occasional mutual crush, but no one stood
around for the true long haul with Tarriona. I wasn't having sex,
so that took a lot of guys out of the game. So, when this guy
came around with all the tricks he had up his sleeve, I just didn't
understand how to play his game. I had never met anyone like
him before. He was beautiful, he didn't pressure intimacy, he
was smart, and he played hard to get. I won't lie, some days he
left me doubting some parts of my beauty. *Why doesn't he want to
hold hands? Why does he push away when we hug too long? Is it me?*
But when it was nighttime, and it was just him and me, he was
different. He was mine.

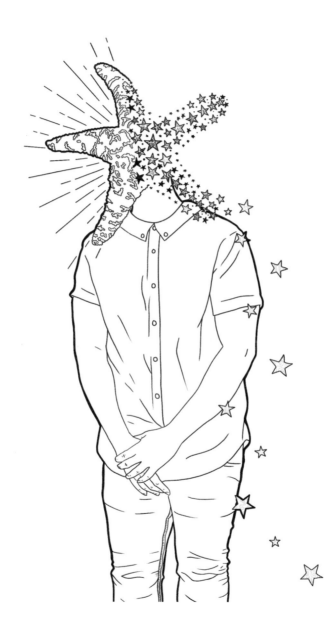

Flashy Fish

You're as selfish as a starfish
You only shine at night when everyone is asleep
You never did admit that you were a star to me
Just a fish
Never knew that you liked to come out at night and put on a show
Until we were out of the water . . . on the road

Survival Guide

When you finally learn the right way to play with fire
You will burn the bridge that constantly brought you back to him
You will notice the vines that you swung on to avoid his mood swings
You will climb them, and you will cut them at the root
Why?

Such a thing will grow back if not severed properly
You will be hungry
Your stomach will no longer feed off the bullshit

You'll realize that it's not as filling as you once thought it was
You will become cold
You will miss his arms
That provided warmth and shelter

You will hear voices
You will see things

Certain pictures will make you remember,

But remember, memories
Only show our favorite scenes

When you finally get off your knees
You will notice the ocean beneath your feet
You will stop drowning when you realize you can breathe through
your tears
You will then understand that you are a survivor in every sense of
the word
And you will no longer need a guide to tell you what you already
know

Could Be Anything

If you were a color
You would be an earth tone
If you were skin
You would have no other choice but to be black
If you were a poem
You would be long and drawn out, sort of like the ones in these pages
If you were a book
You would be an interesting read with a fucked-up ending
If you grew out of the earth
You would be a tall moss tree that gets angry when kids grow up
and don't hang on you anymore
If you were a song
You would surprisingly be a capella
Why? You would prefer to be alone
If you were a test
You would be an essay on a subject no one has ever heard about
If you were mine . . . well, you would have been a long time ago

Tank's Story Time

My Bad

When I first met him, I had a little nickname for him. I would call him "Sun." He was so beautiful to me. Literally tall, dark, and handsome. He was perfect. I would light up with every text, every call, every time I saw him or heard his voice. I even had a little special ringtone for him that sounded like a bunch of drums because it was how my heart felt when he called, and they were also the instrument he played. So, every time I heard those drums, I knew it would be him. And I beamed. It's almost like he started to hate the responsibility of such a nickname, like it moved him away from me instead of drawing him near. It's been so long since I called him that, I wonder if he still remembers how it felt to be someone who made me feel that way.

Sun and Moon Folk

I used to call you Sun
And I, your Moon
We gave each other such important names
So early in the day
Maybe I can see why you turned eclipse

Never thought that the names would become bigger than the sky
that carried them
I guess you
Didn't want the responsibility of brightening my day in that way
Didn't know that you never wanted to gleam like that
But you should know
I didn't call you Sun with the intent for such a responsibility
I called you Sun because when I saw you . . .
I shined

Magnifying Glass

If I took away every drum solo
Every sway of your wooled, thick, onyx hair
Every touch from your long, piano-key fingers
Every glare from the deepest mud puddles I've ever stepped in
Every ridiculous remark that showed your planet was near mine
Or every time you said something that made my mind bend and
change its shape
If it were not for the little things blocking my view of the whole you
I would see something entirely different . . .
I would see you
And not just my favorite parts

Tank's Story Time

Back Up, Bish

It's like a woman has a certain Spidey Sense when she feels another woman is attracted to her man. Or at least I know I do. Call it intuition or the other word that begins with an "I": insecurity.

I would hate when a girl would get too close. I would hate any time another woman saw his gift the way I saw his gift, any time he seemed to show interest in another. It was always my fear that he would find someone who could happily put up with the things that I couldn't seem to let slide. Her success would mean my failure.

Spots That Are Hard to Get Out

Do you know how hard it is to ignore a red spot on a white couch?

To walk past it
Try not to clean it, ignore it
Or treat it like it never existed?

To see a guest sit on it and try to clean it themselves?
Bitch, do not touch my sofa
I'm going to see you tonight
And I will walk past you

If I catch your eyes
I will immediately drop them

You will make sure you stare when no one is watching
And I
Will treat you like the couch

And you will treat me like the stain

Drumsticks

His hands are like drumsticks
Long
Rough
Hard
Delicate
Smooth
Rude
Passionate
I would break if he touched me

Professionals

If I look over my shoulder, I know you'll be there
Breaking when I say break
Listening for the highs and lows in my voice
Perfectly patrolling my cadence
Please . . . only for the songs
My heartbeat doesn't need you to keep its rhythm

Tank's Story Time

Two Monkeys

When I had another job at Winn-Dixie, I worked with Ms. Ann.
Ms. Ann was a divorced woman with four kids, and I looked to
her for advice. She had a funny way of saying things that really
made me listen, like, "two monkeys gon' swing from the same
vine if it can support the two" (referring to a cheater with a big
. . . vine). I remember how she thought I was silly for waiting
around for him. I always wondered if she knew that lessons
weren't learned backwards.

Standing Still

Older Woman: Tarriona! Why would you allow your heartstrings to get so tangled in themselves? How could you be so careless with the kite strings too? My love, you must do better. Mustn't let yourself get "carried" away.

Remember, your feet are to keep those fancy thoughts of yours grounded. Planted.
But that's OK. You'll learn your lesson when your kite gets stuck in a tree. Oh! Maybe you can climb up and get it.

Me: Unless, unless my feet are still planted.

Puzzle Piece

I hate the piece of me that wanted the missing part of you

Libra Thinking

I tried to give you 100 percent honesty
You, in return, gave me sixty-two
Thank you, though

You let me see exactly what I didn't want from anyone—
An imbalance of truth, no matter what form it's in

Tank's Story Time

Take the "L"

There were so many times that I thought about breaking this whole thing off. The arguments, the makeups, the silly fights over different points of view that would last for days. And I mean days! Why weren't we mature? Why couldn't we just rise above it? Why couldn't he just take the "L" . . . why couldn't I? Our egos always felt so much bigger than our love, and we fell into a crazy cycle that we couldn't seem to get out of. I remember one time we had a fight about him asking to use a chair that I was already sitting in. Talk about a world war. I stormed out, he called me selfish, I called him inconsiderate. I got a hotel room. It was truly ridiculous. For some reason, I always think it's better if I walk away from the messes I make, even though when I come back things are exactly as I left them.

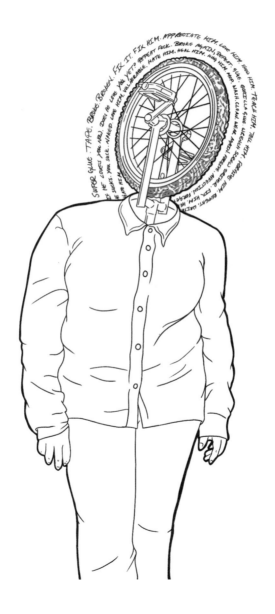

The Cycle

Super glue. Tape. Broke. Broken. Fix it. Fix him. Appreciate
him. Love him. Show him. Teach him. Tell him. Forgive him.
Repeat. Write. Write for him. Sing. Sing for him. See if he loves
you now. Does he love you yet? Repeat. Fuck, broke again, repeat.
Glue. Gorilla glue. Wrench, screwdriver. Fix him. Hearing aid—
what?—damn. This sucks. He sucks. You suck. Naked. Love him.

Vulnerable. Hate him. Heal him. Hug him. Mop. Wash. Clean.
Wear again. Forgive. Affection. Forget. Kiss him. Repeat. Hate
him. Recite. Broke again. Stare at him. Stare at each other. Cry.
Start again. Lock eyes. Find the key. Admit. Confess. Cry. Write.
Feel, breathe. Write. Repeat. And realize: that he was never yours
to fix . . . or heal. Now forgive yourself for pretending to be a
Band-Aid and heal yourself.

Monsters

If you were not so afraid of the monsters in the closet
You would see that they're just clothes in there—
Clothes that you have worn and outgrown

Tank's Story Time

My Business Is Your Business

I'll never forget how complicated the relationship started off. It was at an open mic, and let's just say the wires weren't the only things that were hot that night. I was in love with the way he touched the drum, his movements, and the way he watched me while he played. I asked a mutual friend about him, which ended up being a big mistake. Soon, she became the only way we communicated with each other, because we were too chicken to do it alone.

At the beginning, a regular day would go like this:
"Hey, did you talk to him earlier?"
"Hey, he's looking for you."
"Hey, did you get in touch with him today?"

It started feeling like a relationship, but one that couldn't function without the help of this friend. And, yeah, that was a mess.

Wires

There was a telephone cord in between us
It connected us
Linked us

Didn't matter that it listened to our conversations
Didn't matter that the cord had its own opinions
Didn't matter that it interrupted our speech
All that mattered was that it connected us

It didn't matter that through this wire
Words were jumbled and unclear
That wire began to wrap itself around your neck and mine
Pretty soon, all I heard was the dial tone

Postpone

The day I tell you that I don't wanna do this anymore
Will be the day you believe me
This is why I've been stalling—
I'm waiting to mean it

Expectations

I never thought I expected anything from you
Until the day you hugged me like amnesia
I guess I expected for you to hold me like I was the
Type of thing you could not forget

Maybe I expected too much
Maybe I should have never let your arms
Drive up and down my body
As if they were lost
Looking for a fucking rest stop

Whether it be my body or my heart
Maybe I had too many lights on
Made you feel safe, like I was shelter
The kind of place that you
Hide your boredom in

Don't touch me if you don't mean it

Don't make me feel like some weekend hotel in New Orleans
You're not yourself here
Maybe I was wrong for expecting more from you
And maybe you were wrong
For giving me something to expect

It's not my fault you left your intentions in New Orleans
And picked up Misleading, you carried it in your book sack
People will say that you cannot control your feelings
But your hands...

Your hands are your own

And you didn't just touch me
You held me
You held me like if you let me go, morning would come too soon
As if we only came alive at night

Because soon as the day would hit your back
I would be a stranger to your heart
I would be a foreigner to your eyes

I had no need to wonder how it felt to have a Sun who was
embarrassed by its sky
How dare you make me feel like an eclipse to your shine?
A dark hiding place for your wet dreams
A busy spot for your fingers when they were not busy holding sticks

When morning comes
You will jump, Adam

You will treat me like a friend

And you will visit me while everyone is asleep

I will bend my back to suit your body and you will hold me
Like you should have this evening . . .
When I asked you for a hug
And your arms felt like quiet
Like quick
And I could hear my confidence walk away with an awkward limp
The type of walk ya get
When a motherfucka like you
Likes to trip someone

That's walking towards you with the same body
You held them with
So I'm confused . . .
Was I a punching bag or a pillow?

Dry

I am waiting patiently for the well you built inside of me to dry up
That way
When you are thirsty
I will have nothing to offer you but a dry hole

Tank's Story Time

Tiny Desk

If anybody has ever seen my Tiny Desk concert, you've heard the opening poem, "For the Body, for the Heart." It makes you bop your head, maybe snap your fingers. It probably makes you feel good inside. What I don't talk much about is who I wrote it for.

In my mind, my heart was brand new. Never been used. Never been in love. No past hurt to cling on to. So, when I met the guy that I decided to openly love, it never crossed my mind that he would be apprehensive to receive my love. I started to believe I would be good for him. I wasn't candy, I wasn't pork; I was greens and fish. I would be good for him. I never stopped to think if he would have actually been good for me. My friend told me I should incorporate it into my music, and there it was, "Boxes and Squares," for the world to hear. All ten million.

For the Body, for the Heart

Would have been fish
Would have been meat
Would have been eggs
Would have been greens
Would have been milk
Would have been fruit
Would have been vegetable
Would have been soup
I would have been . . .
Good for you

Tank's Story Time

The Ball Sisters

I have these amazing sisters. Four of us: Anetra, Lashonda, and Tiffany, and of course I'm the baby.

I never had to scrape my knees learning hard lessons, because my sisters were always there to make sure I learned my lessons through them. "Don't have a baby young," "Don't get married too quick!" "Lotion the parts of your body no one can see," "Where is your girdle?" "No, you can't wear your hair out without a perm!" And on love and relationships, where do I begin? The lessons never ended, even to this day!

"Get with someone that loves you more than you love him." "No sex before marriage."
"Don't have too many sexual partners. That's a soul tie."

I had all these lessons protecting me but also hindering me from truly experiencing a fulfilling relationship because I was so scared trying to live up to the women I idolized. To this day, I'm still trying to figure out which lessons I should keep and which ones I should part with.

"You" Stuff

You are smelly hair
That I play in way too much

You are little lips
That I crave more than I should

You are fingers everywhere but the right place
You are stupid-ass art
That I look at for way too long

You're a wet sky
And I've been outside
And now I smell like a dog

You are glasses
That I want off your freaking face

You are eyes that are as deep as neighborhoods drowning in
unsuspected lakes
There should be a warning label on your face
You're an unpleasant combination of sounds
You're cymbals and bass drums
That I listen to too loud

You make me feel like an abusive bitch
Simply because I'm too prideful to ask to touch

I'm nothing but attitude
Pride and excuse
Around you
I'm insecure

And beautiful
Fresh and spoiled
I'm too much but way too little

Often wondered what it would take to get you
Often questioned what she did to capture that heart of yours
Especially since it has been on the run ever since I met it

Glare

Glare (v.): to be unpleasantly bright; to shine brightly and intensely.
You never told me I was beautiful
Never told me I was sexy
Never made me feel like a woman
Never made me feel like a rainbow

Never told me that any of my hair colors complimented my dark
almond eyes
I'm special, ya know
Sometimes I felt like I should tell you
Or maybe show you
That I was everything interesting and colorful
Could not possibly be monochrome
Could not be one color

Will not be sorry for posing as paint
Will not apologize for my shades
Maybe you were color-blind

You will one day have to show me how
You can ignore a dark-skinned rainbow
Because though I was shining right in front of your face
I could not turn my eyes away from yours
So one day
One day
You will have to teach me the art of overlooking the Sun

No Rest

When I wake up, I think about you

In the middle of my day, I wonder about you
And when I go to sleep . . . I dream about you
I just can't seem to get no fucking rest!
Real shit

And, boy, am I tired of this

For someone like you to roam around in my mind
Like a kid at a theme park
If I think about you in my day, can't I at least dream in peace?
Well, it's 5:30 a.m.
I guess that's my answer
Fuck

The Ass

Out of all the parts of the body that you could be

I never thought you, my love, could be the asshole
I thought that maybe you could be hands
Reliable
Soft
There
Holding
Or maybe tongue
Quick
Ready
Smooth
Or perhaps arms
Big
Wide
Strong
Maybe even chest
Broad
Lay
Rest
But of all the things to be, you choose to be an asshole
Shit
Full

And now . . . released

Fishing

My best friend
The person who would not hold his tongue
The person who wants the best for me
The person who wants to see me happy
The person who I once saw my reflection in
Thinks
That we are fishing
He wants me to know
That the worm that you are dangling at the end of your pole
Is glittering, shiny
And fake

Swings

September 3rd
Today, I killed someone
I took the high school girl I used to be
To the back of the playground
And I hung her with the chains from the swings
That your emotions and I used to dangle on
Everyone will say that I killed her, but I think I saved her life . . .

Damaged Merchandise (Walmart)

Attention Walmart shoppers.
Everything in the entire store is free!

But everything in the store is also damaged
Shop at your own risk

I guess you could say I knew what I was buying
I saw you in aisle 4
You were everything broken and beautiful

And I just knew that you would go so well in my heart
I didn't read your warning label
Knew that you had a piece missing
And hazardous things that I could swallow
Like my pride
But I was OK—
You were on sale and you were stunning

I could already see you complementing my art
The painting in the living room of my mind
The tile would go so well with your skin

I could see myself throwing out that old couch me and my ex used
to sit on
You would fit so perfectly in his place
I was ready to make space . . .
As I strolled through the store, I could hear pieces of your honesty
Drop on the floor
I kept walking

I overheard your voice in another aisle

So that let me know, you were communicating with someone else
So I guess we were not communicating
I wondered

How so many pieces of you were missing, yet
You were just as heavy
As the first moment I picked you up from the shelf
I think it's because when I picked you up
I put down myself

Often wondered
How could the same person that made me feel invincible
Treat me like I was invisible
So vulnerable
In your aisle 4
Willing to buy your damaged merchandise just to claim that it was mine and mine alone
Broken and
Beautiful
Torn painting
And here I am making sure I was a beautiful enough frame
Just to hold you

I need to go back to aisle 4
There is a piece of this mirror my mama gave me
I think I left it when I picked up you

Self-reflection should never be confused with who is looking at you
Should have left you where I saw you, but who was I to judge the store in which I was shopping
So should I check the customer or what she was buying?
I walked up to the register

As I was about to check you out
The cashier was your brother
He told me all of your deficiencies

Told me I could not exchange you for another
So I'm sorry; it's my fault
I walked into your Walmart full of explosives, half notes, and torn
notebooks
I put my money on the counter, and I purchased a beautiful
sandstorm

Thank God
I kept my receipt

Just Music

I'm not always gonna feel this way . . . right?
I can already hear the laugh
I can feel the smile tiptoeing across my cheeks
I can see myself not liking you and definitely not loving the
potential
Of something that never was . . .
Soon, all we will make together is music
And I won't expect anything more

Silly Arguments

OK
So maybe I overreacted

Maybe my pride is caught somewhere between your sarcasm
Maybe it hurts a little more when you say it
Maybe our intimacy has ruined you and me and I have never
regretted something so deeply

So, yeah
Maybe I overreacted
Just a little

Wishing Well

Stop looking at me that way

In your face, you have these two deep holes
They are full of everything you're thinking
If I stare too long, I'll fall down those wishing wells
And get lost in pennies and wishes from others
You have a lot of change down here
I'm guessing you have looked into a lot of eyes, inspired a lot of
wishes
And never granted one
Please don't make me just some loose change
So I won't look at you that way if you promise to do the same
This is my only wish

Be Bee

I shouldn't be shocked that your candy is sweeter than usual
Shouldn't give a bee extra attention for doing what he is supposed
to do
He shouldn't get an award for honey that's more syrupy than
normal
Too used to you being bitter, bee
Too used to tasting sour soliloquies
Maybe it was because you got your nectar from
Shy violets and quiet chrysanthemums

Sudden Truth

If I open my chest
Tear the flesh
Break the bone
Untangle the blood vessels
Dismantle the rib cage
And pull out the beat from the heart
I am positive
That I will find your name buried under the deep tissue of my heart

I have no clue why the feelings hold on to something so dead
My pride has been wrangling
My rib cage
To get to the heart to shake it
To wake it the fuck up

I don't know if this will be the last poem I write about you
But it will feel good when I look at it
And laugh

To know that the feelings that I once had
Are nothing but words on a sheet of paper

Adam

(The First Poem I Ever Wrote for Him)

If I suck the air really hard

I could taste your bottom lip

I know exactly what you smell like after you drum

And I still don't mind kissing your forehead, or at least your cheek
In some country, that would probably be considered love

I just wanna kiss the hands that you hold sticks with
Your skin is most beautiful at night
'Cause I like the way it blends in with the dark
And sometimes I like to be on top of you
Just so I can distinguish you from your shadow
Sometimes I want you to stare at me and look at me too
But, then again, I don't want you to notice me staring
I would like to teach you the delicacy of your hands
Remind them that they don't always have to be hard
And intense
Teach them to listen
Rhythm me
Remind them that drums were not always easy
That you had to learn
Before you could hold sticks properly

I like to twist your vines around my branches
I like when your tongue is too thick for your mouth
And you: southern slur your phrases
You don't tell me too many secrets

But when you do . . . I bow-tie them under my tongue
And if you look, I promise you'll find them there

Surprise
I have kept them

I kinda wanna know everything about you

Like the first time she broke your heart, daddy issues, what are you
allergic to?
Do you sleep on your back or your stomach?
Are you near- or farsighted? Are you left- or right-handed?
Right, you're ambidextrous
Do you think I am someone you could fall in love with?
Do you believe we evolved from fish?
Ever wonder if there are other humans on other planets?

Which brings me to my next question . . . do you believe in aliens?

'Cause I've been twisting
And questioning, quoting your phrases
Repeating them backwards
Flipping them forwards and placing them
In my mouth just to see
If it would sound better coming from me

OK, so I've been wondering why you didn't call, and I've been asking
who was that girl
And I been questioning why you ain't texting me back
And I been seeing
You looking only at me, but I'm wondering
How many people have you seen
And I been hoping that all you want is me and for me to be

More than a friend at the same time that I want you to be
So if you're wondering . . . yes, my mind has been on something
No need for assumptions
That something is you
Your secrets smell like laundry on Thursday
You are no longer easy and playful like a puzzle, you are an enigma
of numbers and colors placed on a cliff
Waiting to fall into conundrum

With cymbals, half-written haikus, and bass drums
You are confusing
You make noise; you say nothing
You make me forget reasons why I'm mad at you and pick them up
later
My pride sometimes sits in the back seat when I ride with you but
rides shotgun in the elevator
Going absolutely nowhere
We are not going up
Limbo lazy we saving heaven for later
I wanted my slice now
You wouldn't tell me if you were hungry

All I want to know is why you hide things in your skin knowing how
well your onyx feathers would blend them in
I don't need to know everything you're thinking
But I need to know more than what your lips taste like after midnight
I wanna crack your ex-girlfriend's face open
Wow, that was random
Don't ask me why . . . I just do

I wanna talk to all your ex-girlfriends, see if they all carry the same
big book
Skim through the different chapters, make sure the author is the same

And find out why you weren't so careful with who read you
I'm really eager to read that last chapter
I gotta feeling some of the pages will be ripped out
I gotta feeling that you rip people out of the chapters
I gotta feeling you got a lot of characters
With no leading roles

You write people in your life with pencil
You make sure they are easy to erase
I think you made the mistake before of writing with ink and I don't
think you like that type of permanency
I just wanna ask you . . . who checked you out last
Who tore your cover? Tattered. Ripped.
And leather hard and difficult like scripture

Did they not read in between the lines—
Too many metaphors in your parables?
In your stories, was there a Jezebel?
Masquerading as one of your disciples?

Were you tossed to the side and deemed redundant like the Bible
Did they not read your context clues
Or did you forget to write them?
Were you always this hard to read or
Did someone rewrite you?

Beautiful,
I have always wanted to read someone like you
But I never expected to receive such a borrowed book
I'm still wondering if one of those others
Has a piece of your pages in her left pocket
Maybe with
Some bullshit romance novel or

Her D-minus literary analysis
'Cause she never was good at critical reading

I'll read between your lines
I'll analyze your grammar
I'll do research on your inspiration
And spellcheck your final paper

If I suck the air really hard
I could still taste your bottom lip

I know exactly what you smell like after you drum
And I still don't mind kissing your forehead

Adam
My paper-cut fingers
Would never skim through your pages

When I said I wanted to know all of you
I freaking meant it

Thank you, next

Damn
You have helped create a symphony of similes
With what we made . . . I have created
Thanks

Acknowledgments

I'd like to acknowledge my best friends, Tavia Osbey and Joshua Johnson. Thank you for helping me. I'd also like to acknowledge my publisher, my editor, and my illustrator for giving my feelings a life of their own.

About the Author

Tarriona "Tank" Ball is a New Orleans-based slam poet and Grammy-nominated recording artist with her band, Tank and the Bangas. This is her first book of poetry.

LIVE at LAGUNITAS
#LivedLagunitas
June 27, 2017

TANK AND
THE BANGAS
with
SWEET CRUDE

Praise for Tarriona "Tank" Ball

&

Tank and the Bangas

"Ball is as nimble a lyricist as she is a vocalist, with a malleable voice that's powerful in its command."—*Los Angeles Times*

"New Orleans wordsmith Tarriona "Tank" Ball crafts lyrics that wash over you like secrets between friends: sincere, vulnerable, occasionally hushed, and delightfully dramatic."—*AV Club*

"Lead singer Tank has an elastic, surprising voice that oozes energy, turning simple lyrics into full stories just with a twist of the syllables; perhaps it shouldn't be so unexpected, given her background as a slam poet." —*TIME*

"Tank and the Bangas string together grooves from funk, hip-hop, rock and gospel; serious storytelling, self-empowerment exhortations and dance instructions share the band's exuberant stream of consciousness."—*New York Times*

"There's no leaving a Tank and the Bangas performance in a bad mood."—*New Yorker*

Follow Tank

instagram.com/thinktank20
tankandthebangas.com
youtube.com/user/TankandtheBangas
instagram.com/tankandthebangas
twitter.com/tankanddabangas
facebook.com/TankAndTheBangas

Enjoy *Vulnerable AF* as an audiobook narrated by the author, wherever audiobooks are sold.

Andrews McMeel Publishing
a division of Andrews McMeel Universal
1130 Walnut Street, Kansas City, Missouri 64106

www.andrewsmcmeel.com

21 22 23 24 25 SDB 10 9 8 7 6 5 4 3 2 1

ISBN: 978-1-5248-6575-7

Library of Congress Control Number: 2020950460

Illustrations by Shonté Young-Williams

Editor: Allison Adler
Art Director: Tiffany Meairs
Production Editor: Elizabeth A. Garcia
Production Manager: Tamara Haus

ATTENTION: SCHOOLS AND BUSINESSES
Andrews McMeel books are available at quantity discounts with bulk purchase for educational, business, or sales promotional use. For information, please e-mail the Andrews McMeel Publishing Special Sales Department: specialsales@amuniversal.com.